DATE DUE			
MAY 14 '8?			
NOV 13			

DENMARK

in pictures

Prepared by Toby A. Reiss

VISUAL GEOGRAPHY SERIES

 STERLING PUBLISHING CO., INC.

NEW YORK

 Oak Tree Press Co., Ltd.

London & Sydney

VISUAL GEOGRAPHY SERIES

Afghanistan
Alaska
Argentina
Australia
Austria
Belgium and
   Luxembourg
Berlin
Bolivia
Brazil
Bulgaria
Canada
The Caribbean
Ceylon
   (Sri Lanka)
Chile
China
Colombia
Costa Rica
Cuba
Czechoslovakia
Denmark

Dominican
   Republic
East Germany
Ecuador
Egypt
El Salvador
England
Ethiopia
Fiji
Finland
France
Ghana
Greece
Greenland
Guatemala
Guyana
Haiti
Hawaii
Holland
Honduras
Hong Kong
Hungary

Iceland
India
Indonesia
Iran
Iraq
Ireland
Islands of the
   Mediterranean
Israel
Italy
Ivory Coast
Jamaica
Japan
Jordan
Kenya
Korea
Kuwait
Lebanon
Liberia
Madagascar:
   The Malagasy Republic
Malawi

Malaysia and
   Singapore
Mexico
Morocco
Nepal, Bhutan
   & Sikkim
New Zealand
Nicaragua
Nigeria
Norway
Pakistan
Panama and the
   Canal Zone
Paraguay
Peru
The Philippines
Poland
Portugal
Puerto Rico
Rhodesia
Rumania
Russia

Saudi Arabia
Scotland
Senegal
South Africa
Spain
The Sudan
Surinam
Sweden
Switzerland
Tahiti and the
   French Islands
   of the Pacific
Taiwan
Tanzania
Thailand
Tunisia
Turkey
U.S.A.
Uruguay
Venezuela
Wales
West Germany
Yugoslavia

PICTURE CREDITS

The publishers wish to thank the Standard Oil Company of New Jersey for the photographs used on the following pages: 9 (b), 11 (b), 12 (b), 14 (t), 31, 39, 58 (t), 62 (t). All other photographs were provided by the Information Office of the Royal Danish Ministry for Foreign Affairs, to which grateful acknowledgment is made.

Sixteenth Printing, 1980

Copyright © 1978, 1973, 1972, 1971, 1969, 1966, 1961
by Sterling Publishing Co., Inc.
Two Park Avenue, New York, N.Y. 10016
Distributed in Australia and New Zealand by Oak Tree Press Co., Ltd.,
P.O. Box J34, Brickfield Hill, Sydney 2000, N.S.W.
Distributed in the United Kingdom and elsewhere in the British Commonwealth
by Ward Lock Ltd., 116 Baker Street, London W.1
Manufactured in the United States of America
All rights reserved
Library of Congress Catalog Card No.: 61-10396
Sterling ISBN 0-8069-1002 –X Trade   Oak Tree 7061– 6009 6
1003 –8 Library

Denmark's famous Tivoli.

CONTENTS

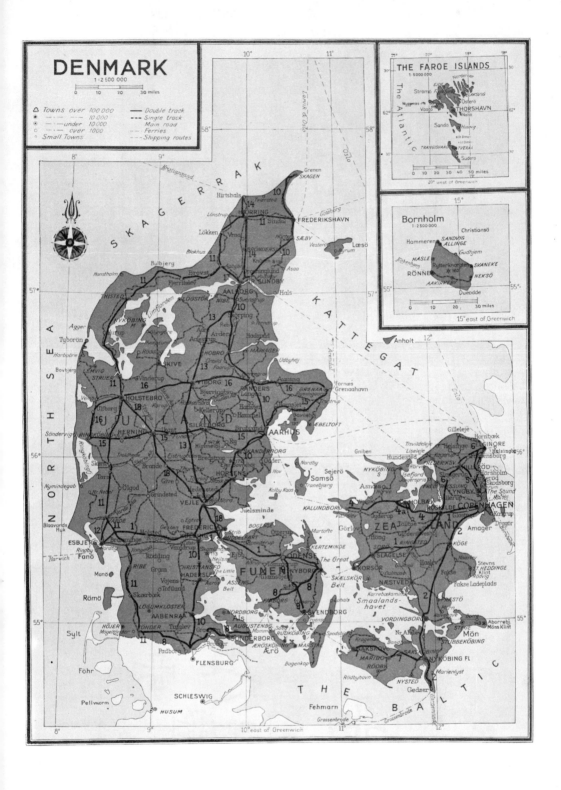

DENMARK

1:2 500 000

0   10   20   30 miles

△ Towns over 100 000
⊙ — 10 000
⊛ — under 10 000
⊙ — over 1000
∘ Small Towns

━━━ Double track
┄┄┄ Single track
━━━ Main road
┅┅┅ Ferries
─·─·─ Shipping routes

THE FAROE ISLANDS

1:5 000 000

The Atlantic

Norderøer
Strømø Østerø
Mygganes Vaagø THORSHAVN
Nalsø
Sandø
Hvannø

TRANGISVAAG TVERAA
Suderø

0   10   20   30   40   50 miles

20° west of Greenwich

Bornholm

1:2 500 000

Hammeren   Christiansø
SANDVIG
Allinge
Hasle   Gudhjem
Rytterknægten SVANEKE
RÖNNE ✠162
NEKSÖ
AAKIRKEBY
Dueodde

0   10   20   30 miles

15° east of Greenwich

INTRODUCTION

Denmark is an enchanting country of lakes and fjords, sandy beaches beyond which are hills containing the burial mounds of ancient Vikings, a country of dense woods, fields upon fields of soft heather, of neatly laid out farms and clean villages where the smell of salt water is always in the air. Denmark is the oldest kingdom in Europe, and the country has retained an atmosphere of Viking conquests long past.

Denmark's most representative figure is Hans Christian Andersen, who wove many whimsical tales for the pleasure of children—and adults—everywhere. Today a statue of his Little Mermaid sits wistfully on a rock in the port of Copenhagen; she is a reminder to Danes and visitors alike that Denmark is still a land of fairy tales.

Each evening the lights of Tivoli, the splendid combination amusement park-theatrical area, shine brightly in every hue imaginable, while nearby the clock at the Rådhus (or City Hall) plays a tune before it strikes the hour. Tivoli symbolizes the dreamlike aspect of Denmark. Among the twinkling lights and flower-lined walks and parks of Tivoli, children find even more pleasures than in dreams. If they like, they can ride in state in a handsome coach-and-four, or take a whirl on any one of many rides designed especially for them by Denmark's leading architects. Perhaps they will visit the pantomime theatre, the Flea Circus or the House of Forbidden Games, where children are permitted to do many things not allowed at home—climbing trees, for example, or writing on walls.

Perhaps every Dane has something of Hans Christian Andersen in his nature. But if this is true, the Danes have not allowed their love of the imaginary and the pleasurable to make them impractical. They are hard-working people, more than capable of meeting the challenges posed by their country's geographic limitations and by the economic obstacles facing a small nation. Even though Denmark has few raw materials, this old but modern kingdom is meeting the world's competition with remarkable success. Its agricultural products, industrial exports, handicrafts and flair for modern design have won respect the world over. Inborn ingenuity is the most outstanding trait of Denmark's people.

In this book you will learn how the Danes won an empire and clung to it tenaciously for several centuries before assuming a position of neutrality in world affairs. You will see, too, how these determined people have made the most of a land poor in agricultural and industrial resources, how a unique educational system was developed many years before similar systems were established in other countries, how Danish athletes, writers and musicians have used their talents to add to the fame of their country.

Through pictures you will visit villages and towns, and explore Copenhagen, Denmark's medieval island capital, a city of varied and striking architectural beauty and of a distinct poetic atmosphere. Above all, Copenhagen is the site of Tivoli, that fairyland so long remembered by those who see it in pictures as well as by those fortunate enough to visit Denmark in person.

For centuries, Danish beech trees have been praised by the poets of the country. Around May 1st, when the beeches burst into leaf and the ground is covered with millions of white anemones, city dwellers go to the country to enjoy the beautiful sight.

I. THE LAND

It comes as a surprise to many to realize that the kingdom of Denmark is not self-contained, but is scattered in the North and Baltic Seas. The land consists of the peninsula of Jutland, which separates the North Sea from the Baltic, and some 500 islands—about 100 of which are inhabited. These islands provide wonderful natural facilities for shipping and fishing. The total area of the country is 16,619 square miles. It is a low-lying country, the highest point being 570 feet above sea level. Southernmost of the Scandinavian countries, its only land boundary is with Germany, which adjoins the Danish mainland of Jutland on the south. The Strait of Skagerrak separates it from Norway on the north, and the Strait of Kattegat divides it from Sweden on the east.

The most notable islands are Zealand, Fünen and Falster. Copenhagen, the largest city and capital, is on Zealand, and is the only European capital situated on an island. Denmark is truly a land of bridges, for these connect many of its islands. Other parts of the country are united by ferries and coastal ships—and since no Dane lives more than about 30 or 40 miles from the coast, Jutland is easily accessible from any of the main islands. In summer, modern passenger ships provide quick transportation between Copenhagen, the "Paris of Scandinavia," and large Jutland towns. Every 24 hours these ships make two 7-hour trips.

Denmark also has two overseas possessions. One is Greenland, the largest island in the world, located between Canada and Iceland and lying almost entirely within the Arctic Circle. It measures 840,000 square miles, but almost seven-eighths of Greenland consists of barren mountains, covered with ice as thick as 8,000 feet in some places. The other overseas possession is the Faroes, a group of 19 volcanic islands (18 of which are inhabited) in the Atlantic, northwest of Scotland.

Denmark, "the field of the Danes," is very aptly named, for it is a land of small farms. These constitute about 75 per cent of the country. The panorama of the land is peaceful and harmonious, with its undulating green fields neatly squared, and its abundance of serene lakes reflecting the myriad handsome beech trees. (Approximately 10 per cent of Denmark is taken up by forests, planted to

Storks nest on the roof of the cathedral of Ribe in Jutland. A century ago, 10,000 of the birds arrived in Denmark every spring to nest, returning in autumn to their winter homes in Africa. In 1970, only 70 pairs were counted!

Agricultural Denmark, the supplier of quality foods to the western world, is serene and attractive. Although farming is an ancient occupation, today the fields and farms are cultivated according to efficient, modern methods.

hold down the soil of the heaths by combatting strong winds.)

The land itself presents few sharp contrasts. The western regions of Jutland are composed of stretches of sand, where vigorous grasses have been planted to keep the land from being washed away by the sea. Here on the hills by the shores are large circular mounds—remnants of days long past; these are the burial mounds of ancient chieftains from the Viking Age. Beyond the sand hills, the land is flat. Once this area was a barren, wind-swept heath covering a large portion of Jutland, but today it is almost entirely cultivated. One of the oldest towns of Denmark, located on Jutland, is Ribe, a small, dike-protected village renowned for its many storks. But despite the abundance in nearby marshes of frogs and lizards on which storks feed, these comical birds are slowly diminishing in number. During winter storks migrate to South Africa, where, unfortunately many are killed.

Fünen, the most charming of the Danish islands, is shaped somewhat like a heart, set protectively between two arms of the sea called the Little Belt and the Great Belt. It is sheltered by Zealand on the east, and Jutland on the west and northwest. The provincial capital of Fünen is Odense, Denmark's third largest city and the birthplace of its beloved storyteller, Hans Christian Andersen. In the southwest, above a blue fjord—a narrow inlet of the sea nestling between high rocks—and just below gently rolling green hills—sometimes referred to as the "Fünen Alps"—is the picturesque resort Faaborg, an old town that has been sketched hundreds of times by visiting artists.

On the island of Möen, steep, snow-white cliffs reach upward, and all over the kingdom, the rivers of the different islands wind through vast beech woods and into beautiful, serene fjords.

CLIMATE

Unlike the landscape where there are few striking extremes, the Danish climate varies greatly. The winters may be surprisingly mild, although rather grey and cloudy, or the seas

Above: One of the most charming aspects of Denmark is the frequent contrast between the old and the new. This farmer may have his milk churned by the most modern dairy methods in the world, but he still prefers a sturdy straw-thatched roof on his farmhouse to tile or slate. A straw roof helps keep the house warm in winter, and cool in summer. It lasts for many years, but if it needs replacing, there are plenty of farmers nearby who know just how to do it.

On the tiny island of Manö, about 4 miles off the coast of Jutland, bundles of long grass lie in a pile. They will be used for repairing the thatched roof of the distant farmhouse.

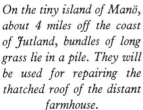

The Faroe Islands consist of basalt rocks formed by volcanic activity. Their volcanic origin has given the islands their characteristic rocky appearance. Sheer cliffs of dark basalt are broken up by layers of reddish turf—deposits of volcanic ash.

and fjords may be completely covered with ice, making travel difficult. But with cold winds blowing off the northern ice in winter, the temperature usually drops to freezing and sometimes below for about 100 frosty days.

In summer, the average temperature is about 61°—mild and temperate. Danes go swimming from May to September, although the water would probably seem a bit chilly to others. The sun shines for a total of about 2 months each year and there is often a soft drizzling rain to keep the fields green and the streets glistening.

Twilight nights, sometimes called "white nights," start on May 8 and end on August 8. During this period the light of the "Midnight

Above: This little girl is playing on the coast of the rocky little island of Bornholm, some 225 square miles in area. It is situated about 93 miles from Copenhagen, in the Baltic. Though small in area, the island is rich in scenic variety. Steep cliffs, rolling fields, and wide beaches are set among sand dunes. One of the largest forests in Denmark is on Bornholm. Rönne, with nearly 12,000 inhabitants, is the island's largest town.

Right: An intriguing feature of the Danish coast is this road that runs along the bottom of the sea. During ebb tide, the sea between the mainland (Jutland) and Manö can be crossed by automobile or by cart, by following a track marked by dead trees. The path is usable 6 hours a day, but during high tide, it is covered by 5 feet of water.

This is a herring smokehouse in the seaside village of Allinge - Sandvig on Bornholm.

A huge, old-fashioned windmill still stands on the island of Aero, in the Little Belt, south of Fünen.

Right: Among the attractions of Bornholm, are four peculiar "round" churches—each a fortress and church combined. They were built more than 800 years ago. This is St. Oluf's Church, or Kirke.

Sun" shines around the clock above the Arctic Circle and brightens even the southernmost parts of Scandinavia far into the night, covering everything with a soft, misty haze. The Danes celebrate this spectacle on Midsummer's Eve, June 23rd, by building bonfires in the cool summer evenings. And sun-worshippers crowd the hillsides on Whitsunday (the seventh Sunday after Easter) to see the sun come up, just 3 hours after midnight.

Below: Denmark has many excellent wayside inns. Most of them are picturesque with thatched roofs to emphasize their old-fashioned charm. This is Sölleröd Inn near Copenhagen.

Above: Ferries play an important part in Denmark's transportation system. There are 23 ferries operated by the Danish State Railway plus a number of private ones, some connecting islands within Denmark, and others making trips to Sweden and Germany. Scandinavians do not have to show passports to travel between their own countries.

Left: In the past it was troublesome to cover long distances because the traveller had to change several times between train and ferry. Now, however, there are bridges connecting the larger islands as well as Jutland and Fünen. This is the Storstrom Bridge between Zealand and the island of Falster.

*Entrance to
Christiansborg Palace*

2. THE HISTORY OF DENMARK

Strange as it seems, idyllic, unmilitary, peaceful Denmark was once a vast and powerful empire that included England and Norway within its domain. During certain periods between the 11th and 15th centuries, Denmark ruled over an area twice as large as that of any kingdom in Europe.

This rise to power started in the Viking Age, a 300-year period beginning in the 9th century, in which all the Scandinavian countries have common roots. The Danish and Norwegian Vikings conquered England, controlled the North Sea, created small kingdoms in Ireland,

established colonies in Normandy, and sailed the coasts of western Europe, defeating power after power. Meanwhile, the Swedish Vikings were spreading through Russia and down to the Caspian and Black Seas. Vikings even reached America 500 years before Columbus. The causes of their many raids are obscure, but overpopulation is known to be one of them. Although these Vikings were primarily seamen and shipbuilders, pirates, adventurers and traders, they mastered the arts of colonization and government, too.

Denmark is the oldest nation in the world

today with a government nominally ruled by a king or queen. Nobody knows exactly how long ago the kingdom was formed, but Gorm the Old is the first sovereign about whom there are any facts. It is not known where or when he was born, or when he ascended the throne, but there are records of his death around 950. Gorm and his wife, Thyra Danebrod, are buried at Jellinge in Jutland where their son, Harold Bluetooth, erected stone monuments in their memory. One of the stones bears a carved picture of the crucifixion and claims that Gorm made Denmark and Norway Christian countries. Ansgar, a French monk, had appeared in Denmark in 826. He was the first to preach the Christian religion to the Danes. Previously, they had worshipped pagan gods, the most important being Odin, Freya and Thor.

Christianity did not end the raids of the Vikings. Although Harold Bluetooth accepted it, he continued his raids along with his son, Sweyn Forkbeard. Together they attacked England many times, in 994 besieging London with some 90 ships. Sweyn also partitioned parts of Norway.

It remained for Sweyn's son, Canute II, later known as "the Great," to consolidate the lands won by his father and grandfather. By 1016 he had conquered all of England, which was governed by Danish kings until 1042, and by 1028 he had become the ruler of Norway as well. Canute the Great, a wise militarist, diplomat and administrator, was readily accepted both by the English and by the Norwegians. He was a sincere Christian, and while in England, sent many bishops back to strengthen

This replica of a sturdy yet graceful Viking ship is taking part in the annual Viking Festival at Frederikssund. Many actual relics of these ships are still found along the coast. The Danish National Museum is preparing to raise seven such ships, sunk 1,000 years ago and recently discovered almost intact in Roskilde Fjord, Zealand.

Christiansborg Palace in Copenhagen houses the parliament, the ministry of foreign affairs, the supreme court and the royal reception rooms. In the foreground is a statue of Bishop Absalon who founded Copenhagen on this spot in 1166.

the church in Denmark. Once consolidated, Canute's kingdom prospered in peace. However, after his death England and Norway became separated from the Danish kingdom, Norway, however, only temporarily. Perhaps one of Denmark's greatest kings, Canute was, oddly, buried in England's Winchester Cathedral. The empire he had created crumbled within a few short years.

There is a folk-tale about Canute. One day he ordered his servants to carry him in his royal chair and robes to the edge of the beach in England. As he sat there, the tide began to come in and the waves threatened to wet his robes. In all his majesty, he rose and pointing at the beach commanded the tide to "rise thus far and no farther." Of course, the tide rose and wet his feet, proving that he was not all-powerful.

Although the rulers who followed King Canute the Great tried to build up the Danish kingdom, it was not until the reign of Valdemar I, beginning in 1157, that Denmark became a civilized country, consolidated internally. Cities were founded, churches built and much of the land cleared of forests, giving agriculture a chance to develop. Valdemar I is the only Danish sovereign besides Canute II to bear the title of "Great." But he would not have achieved all that he did without the help of one of the great personalities of the Middle Ages—Bishop Absalon. Valdemar had spent most of his childhood on Absalon's father's estate on Zealand, and so they were close friends. Since Absalon had studied theology in Paris, his knowledge of the outside world was invaluable to Denmark. Together Absalon and Valdemar set out to restore the country that had been wracked by civil wars and oppressed by unjust taxation. To stimulate prosperity and to build a loyal army, Valdemar permitted any Dane who could fully equip himself for military service at his own expense to become a noble, therefore exempt from paying taxes on his estate.

Absalon attended to military affairs as well as to those of the Church. He warred successfully against the Wends, the people of eastern Germany who were continually plaguing the Danes. Then he founded Copenhagen in 1166 as a coastal fortress, strengthened the defences of the east coast, levied taxes for the building of ships, and added to Denmark's holdings parts of northern Germany. Education spread, churches and monasteries appeared by the scores and half the cities of present-day Denmark sprang up. With the help of Absalon, Valdemar the Great ruled in peace for 25 years.

The next 400 years, however, were characterized by frequent changes of national boundaries, by chaos caused by a struggle for supremacy among the royalty, the nobility and the Church and by an external struggle between the Scandinavian countries and the states of present-day Germany. Disputes over German Holstein and Schleswig plagued Denmark until the late 19th century.

Although Valdemar's second son, Valdemar the Victorious (who ruled from 1202-1241), added to the Danish sovereignty parts of Prussia, Estonia, Pomerania and Holstein, political confusion became rampant after his death. Supported by Holstein, the dukes of Schleswig seized control of their area and attempted to overthrow the Danish kings, simultaneously involved in contests for power with the archbishops of Denmark. The kingdom was bankrupt and without a king for 8 years; it was not until 1340 that order was restored.

In that year, Valdemar IV, a dynamic man filled with love for Denmark, was placed on the throne. To consolidate the kingdom, Valdemar married a princess of Holstein and engaged his 7-year-old daughter to marry the son of the Swedish king. Valdemar further strengthened Denmark by taking Visby, the main trading base of the Hanseatic League, a trade monopoly established by 70 or 80 cities of northern Europe for protection against piracy and foreign competition. The base of Baltic trade was transferred from Visby to Copenhagen where it flourished despite resistance from the German states for more than a century.

Nevertheless, the persistent struggle between the Germans and the Scandinavians over land and trade continued, even through the comparatively peaceful reign of Margaret, the only woman who ever ruled over the Danes.

The ruins of Absalon's fortress, built in the 12th century for defence against pirates, still exist under Christiansborg Palace. Saxo Grammaticus wrote his "Historia Danica" here; Shakespeare later used it as a source for his "Hamlet."

This solid Round Tower was built by Christian IV to serve as an astronomical observatory, and also as a tower to the adjoining Church of the Trinity. A spiral causeway leads to the summit, broad enough for a coach and pair. Legend tells that Peter the Great of Russia actually drove to the top in a coach when he visited Copenhagen in 1716.

Margaret became Queen of Denmark in 1387 after the death of her son Olav V, the grandson of Valdemar IV. A shrewd woman, often compared to Queen Elizabeth I of England, Margaret was a skilled diplomat, managing to reverse many difficult situations to her gain. After her husband the King of Norway died, she became the ruler of that country and, later, of Sweden as well. At their request, she helped the Swedes overthrow their unpopular and incompetent sovereign. Afterwards she called a conference at Kalmar, Sweden, in 1397 to bind the three countries together. Although Norway remained part of Denmark until 1814, Sweden many times attempted to break away and in 1520 was successful. None of the sovereigns who followed Margaret had the power or the shrewdness to hold the Scandinavian empire together.

In 1448 the house of Oldenburg, a former German line from which the present Danish king is descended, came into power with Christian I. He brought the German states of Holstein and Schleswig once more under Danish control. Since his reign, all the Danish kings, except one (King Hans) have taken the name of Christian or Frederik.

During the reigns of Christian II, III and IV, and Frederik I, II and III, the years between 1513 and 1670, war characterized Denmark's history. After the "Blood Bath of Stockholm" conducted by Christian II in 1520, Sweden seceded from the kingdom of Denmark-Norway. Later involving his country in the Thirty Years' War, Christian IV attempted to regain Sweden, but succeeded only in losing part of Norway and leaving Denmark in a state of destruction. Its fleet was ruined, its trade seriously damaged, and the levying of heavy taxes caused rebellion.

These constant wars were a serious setback to the economic and social development of

Christian IV, nicknamed the "Sailor King," always solicitous about the welfare of his seamen, built Nyboder, a row of charming yellow houses near Copenhagen's port. Now, more than three centuries later, retired sailors of the Royal Danish Navy still live in these agreeable clean quarters.

Denmark, for until the disastrous effects of the Thirty Years' War, the kingdom had prospered, partly because the Protestant Reformation had successfully broken the secular power of the Roman Catholic Church. Lutheranism is still the state religion of Denmark. Revenue from the confiscated lands of the Roman Catholic Church enabled the monarchy and the nobility to erect many buildings and to lay the groundwork for economic growth. Although this prosperity was completely destroyed by wars with Sweden and Germany during the reign of Christian IV, Frederik III (1648-1670) did much to restore peace and harmony in his kingdom.

Supported by the Lutheran Church and the newly growing merchant class, King Frederik was able to subdue the nobles and to extract desperately needed taxes from them. In turn, the landowners were empowered to tax the peasants, who still lived in a condition of serfdom. Farmers' sons, by a system of "privileged villeinage" or *Stavnsbaand*, belonged to the owners of the land on which they were born, and their services were sold by one landowner to another with frequency. Although the peasants had small plots of land for their own use, their responsibilities to their landlord were so great that they seldom had time or energy to cultivate their own property.

The year 1800 is a crucial one in Denmark's history, for it marks the beginning of its present-day liberalism and its effort to maintain neutrality in world affairs. In 1800 the abolition of the *Stavnsbaand* became effective. A bank was established to assist farmers in buying their own land. And although Denmark continued to have severe economic problems during most of the 19th century, agriculture has flourished since 1870. Education reforms were introduced in 1841, a radical measure for the times. Led by N.F.S. Grundtvig, who established Denmark's famous Folk High Schools, agricultural workers have steadily gained in economic strength and in political influence.

The 19th century brought still other political and social reforms to Denmark. One of these was freedom of the press. Another was the introduction in 1841 of free compulsory education. The third and perhaps most important measure was political. In 1849 King Frederik VII yielded to the will of the people, particularly expressed by new rebellions in the duchies of Schleswig and Holstein, and accepted a change from absolute to constitutional monarchy.

Today Denmark's social legislation is among the most advanced in the world. Since the basic laws were introduced, a whole structure has been built to provide security for the Danish people. Each year, the government spends 35

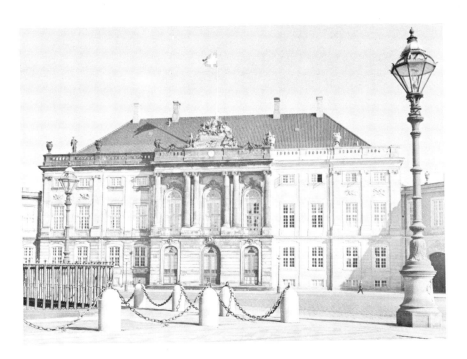

Above: The heart of historical Copenhagen is octagonal Amalienborg Square, surrounded by four rococo palaces, one shown here. When Frederik V donated the ground in 1750 to the four noblemen who wanted to build these palaces, he stipulated that they employ the same architects and adhere to the same style. Today Amalienborg is the official winter residence of the royal family.

Below: Every day, at high noon, Copenhageners can watch the changing of the royal guard at Amalienborg Palace. First the relief guard marches to the palace. Once the guard has changed, with much saluting and flashing of officers' swords, a band assembles under the King's windows, and gives a brief midday concert. When the music is over, the Danish flag is ceremoniously raised.

21

A local artist is shown in Nyhavn, a section of Copenhagen's large port area, busily sketching the anchor monument erected to the memory of Danish seamen. Of the 5,000 Danish seamen who served the Allies in World War II, some 1,400 lost their lives.

Kronborg or Elsinore (Helsingör) Castle built by Frederik II on Kattegat Strait, 28 miles north of Copenhagen, is within sight of Sweden, 3 miles away. It is here that many present-day performances of "Hamlet" are given. Built in Dutch Renaissance style, the castle is surrounded by a moat and high walls.

All over Denmark many castles are still standing. This is the 115-foot-high Goose Tower of Vordingborg Castle, dating back to the 12th century and to Denmark's struggle for independence of the Hanseatic States. The grounds surrounding the castle have been turned into a botanical garden.

to 40 per cent of its budget on the people's welfare, including health, education and social insurance.

Although Denmark made rapid advances politically, economically and socially during the 19th century, it lost great amounts of land as well as the status of a major European power. It tried desperately to remain neutral during the Napoleonic Wars, but in 1801 Lord Nelson and his fleet sailed into Copenhagen port and opened fire. Against their will, the Danes were drawn into the war, naturally on the side of England's enemy, France. As a result, in 1814 Denmark lost Norway to Sweden, but retained the Faroe Islands, which were a dependency of Norway. Still later, Denmark relinquished Schleswig and Holstein to Prussia, a loss representing one-third of its territory and two-fifths of its people.

Again during World War I, Denmark attempted to remain neutral and afterwards relied on the League of Nations to support its position. Once more, after the weakening of the League in the 1930's, Denmark restated its position of strict neutrality. And once more it was drawn into war against its will. In spite of a nonaggression pact of 1939, Germany attacked Denmark in April, 1940, and occupied the country. This marked the beginning of several years of struggle, during which the Germans increasingly usurped political power, harassed and persecuted the Danes in spite of their original promise not to interfere with Denmark's political sovereignty. Denmark's people retaliated by repeated acts of sabotage and a solid attitude of resistance, but in August, 1943, Germany seized the Danish government.

Denmark was liberated, along with the rest of occupied Europe, in 1945. In 1949 it joined NATO and, today, contributes to the United Nations Emergency Forces.

In 1971, negotiations began with the Common Market countries for Danish admission to their economic union, along with England and Ireland. All three countries were admitted on January 1, 1973.

Above: The island inhabitants of Fanö and Amager are especially fond of wearing their national dress for festivals. This procession of young men is riding through Dragor, a small town in Amager, carrying the "Dannegrog," the red and white flag of Denmark.

Right: Fredensborg, meaning "peace castle," was built to commemorate the peace treaty of 1720 which put an end to the territorial conflict between Denmark and Sweden. It lies in poetic Gribskov Forest in Zealand, and is still used by the royal family as an occasional residence. It can be visited, however, at other times, and the fine park which surrounds the castle is open to the public all year round.

This statue of Frederik VII, under whom Denmark's absolute monarchy came to an end in 1848, is appropriately silhouetted against the spires of Christiansborg Castle which now houses the "Folketing."

3. THE GOVERNMENT

In 1848, inspired by the concepts of liberty, equality and fraternity which were the ideals of the French Revolution, the Danes demanded an end to absolute monarchy. A marching delegation advanced on the royal palace and presented their wishes to King Frederik VII. "The King must not drive the nation to the desperation of taking the law in its own hands," the delegation warned.

Without any argument, the King acquiesced to the people's desire that from then on the country would be ruled by their representatives. In accordance with Danish temperament, Denmark's "revolution" was accomplished without bloodshed. On June 5, 1849, a new democratic constitution was drafted. Changes made in 1915 have further extended and strengthened its democratic character.

Today, Denmark's government broadly resembles the British parliamentary system. Like the Queen of England, the Danish Queen "can do no wrong," but as in Great Britain, she exercises her authority only through her ministers and functions primarily as an adviser. The queen has the executive power; the legislative power is vested jointly in the queen and in parliament (*Rigsdag*); the judicial power resides with the courts. This means that although parliament can make and pass laws, no new law can take effect unless the queen has

25

given it her signature. The one action the queen can take independently of parliament is to seek a political leader to form a new government in the event of the current government's resignation. Even this action is taken only after consultation with party leaders. The queen is not permitted to declare war or to sign treaties without the approval of the *Rigsdag*.

In one important respect the Danish parliament differs from that of Great Britain. Although it formerly had two houses, today Denmark's parliament only has one chamber, known as the *Folketing*. Parliament is voted into office for a period of 4 years by universal suffrage of everyone 23 years of age and over. The *Folketing* has 179 members, two of which represent the Faroe Islands, and two of which represent Greenland.

Another major difference between the British and Danish forms of government is that Denmark has a multiple- rather than a two-party system. The present government, for example, is a coalition of the Social Democratic Party, the Social Liberal Party, and the Single-

Tax Party, the three parties combined having a total of 93 seats out of 179. The largest of these is the Social Democratic Party, with 70 seats. This party derives its main support from wage earners, small tradespeople and farmers.

Because of the multiple-party system, the prime minister has a much harder task staying in office than he would if there were only two parties. When any one of his measures meets

The graceful spires of Rosenborg Palace (in the foreground) seem dwarfed by the surrounding museums—the National Art Gallery, the Mineralogical Museum and (on the left) an observatory. But this gay, rose-tinted palace, completed in 1633 by King Christian IV, holds as many treasures as any museum. Its collection of the possessions of Danish kings contains more than 9,900 items. Room after room pours forth a mass of priceless jewels, crowns and even thrones. Perhaps the most magnificent exhibit of all is the tall octagonal case of crown jewels. The treasures of Rosenborg Palace belong to the people of Denmark.

If you walk or cycle through the streets of Copenhagen, you may pass the royal family, either taking a walk or pedalling along on bikes. The royal family joins in the pleasant daily life of the capital without fanfare or fuss, and Copenhageners do not spoil this camaraderie by collecting in crowds or making a commotion when royalty appears. Here (from right to left), shortly after the engagement of Princess Margrethe to Count Henri de Monpezat, are Princess Benedikte, the late King Frederik IX, Queen Ingrid, Princess (now Queen) Margrethe, Count Henri, and members of the Monpezat family.

opposition, the *Folketing* can pass a vote of "no confidence" against him, and he must either resign or demand a new election. In Denmark, a prime minister seldom stays in power the full 4 years.

The Danish monarchy is hereditary. King Frederik married Ingrid, daughter of the King of Sweden and had three daughters.

A constitutional revision of June 5, 1953, was especially promulgated, amending the law of succession so that now a woman, Princess Margrethe, the oldest daughter of King Frederik, could succeed to the throne. In 1967, Princess Margrethe married the French Count Henri de Monpezat, who was given the title of Prince Henrik of Denmark. In January, 1972, King Frederik died and Margrethe succeeded him.

This 1969 photograph of Queen Margrethe and Prince Hendrik, with their two little sons, shows the easy informality of Danish royalty.

Left:
The elaborate interior of the King's Library in Christiansborg Castle contains two surprises. Behind fake bookcases is a hidden staircase; in the front part of the room is an elevator-operated chair that can ascend to the floor above. In this castle are also housed the parliament and government offices.

Right:
One of the display rooms of Rosenborg Castle contains a throne of solid silver, which is guarded by three kittenish, life-like lions, also cast in silver by the famous sculptor Ferdinand Keublich.

Copenhagen's bustling City Hall is the hub of the city. Surrounding it are fine shops, restaurants and film theatres, and close by are the Tivoli Gardens. The City Hall spire rises 350 feet above the square and is an excellent point from which to view the city. Above the main entrance of the City Hall stands a copper statue of Bishop Absalon. Inside is the "World Clock," a famous astronomical clock that is regulated with great precision; it is considered unlikely that it will either gain or lose one single second within the next 750 years. As well as keeping time this clock charts the courses of the sun, planets and stars.

One of the most beautiful buildings in Copenhagen is the Bourse, which is more than 300 years old. Its tower tapers into a spire, formed by the entwined tails of four dragons. The roof is of greenish copper—a masterpiece built by Christian IV. Tuborg's wagons, with their sunshades and horses wearing red and green straw hats, are a popular target for photographers.

4. THE PEOPLE OF DENMARK

The Danes are the most cosmopolitan of all Scandinavians, with one-fourth of their 5,130,000 people residing in Copenhagen, the "Paris of Scandinavia." Another fourth live in provincial towns such as Frederiksberg, Aarhus and Odense. The rest of the population is rather evenly distributed throughout the country on farms, forest plantations, and in fishing villages. The density of the population is about 302 people per square mile—much less than in Belgium or Holland.

For the most part, the Danes live up to our concept of them. Most *are* blond, blue- or green-eyed and fair-skinned—but not any more or less so than other Scandinavians. Hamlet was apparently the only "melancholy Dane." The people of Denmark are vigorous and handsome, generous with hospitality and friendship.

Another similarity among Scandinavians is their language. The Danish language is an offshoot of a Germanic group that evolved from the Viking era, but it has remained very close to the other Scandinavian tongues. Danish,

Norwegian and Swedish are close enough to each other to be easily understood by speakers of each. And although Finnish belongs to a language group akin to Hungarian, most Finlanders also speak Swedish. English is widely spoken in all of Scandinavia.

The original religion of the Scandinavians is known to us through a work of the early 13th century called the *Younger,* or *Prose Edda.* Although it was intended as a handbook of poetics, this book tells us that the pre-Christian Scandinavians worshipped a family of gods who lived at Asgard, in the middle of the earth, in order to protect the humans they had created from being harmed by a race of evil giants. It is believed that these giants represented the more violent forces of nature. Chief of the Norse gods was Odin, who protected warriors; he was also the wind god, the leader of the souls of the dead and the god of magic and poetry. His wife Frigg, as well as another goddess called Freya, represented love, fertility and beauty. Another important god was Thor, the son of Odin, thought to have been

This table is set with the great variety of dishes included in a Danish "smoerre-broed." This expansive meal is offered aboard the ferry that provides transportation between Zealand and Fünen.

Fireworks light up the sky over the light-silhouetted buildings of Tivoli.

In Copenhagen's famous 20-acre Tivoli Gardens as many as 50,000 people can enjoy themselves on a summer evening. Every kind of amusement is to be found here: symphony concerts, performances by acrobats, rides, restaurants, and theatres. Shown here is the outdoor pantomime theatre.

more highly revered than his father in some parts of Scandinavia. It was his special duty to protect mankind from the fierce giants. Our days of the week come from the names of the Norse gods: for example, Friday from Frigg and Thursday from Thor.

Although Denmark was a Roman Catholic country, like the rest of Europe during the Middle Ages, its people accepted the Protestant Reformation. Today the Evangelical Lutheran Church is the national church of Denmark—the king must be a Lutheran. Ninety-eight per cent of the population belong to this denomination, but other religious communities exist. These include the Swedish Church, the Orthodox Russian congregation, the Church of England, the Roman Catholic Church, the Reformed Church, the Methodist Church and the Jewish community.

Again, there is nothing "melancholy" about Danes. They seem to love life more than any other people in the world. One of their great interests is good food. And there are three basics for a fine meal—*smoerrebroed* (literally meaning "smeared bread"), *snaps* and *snak*. *Smoerrebroed* is the Danish version of a sandwich

—but what a sandwich! It is probably closer to the Swedish smorgasbord. Only one fairly thin slice of bread is used; it is buttered, then laden with smoked salmon, tongue, ham, eggs or cheese, and finally trimmed with herbs and pickles. A *smoerrebroed* is a complete meal. But no meal in Denmark is complete without a bit of strong spirits, and this is where the *snaps* comes in. The *snak*, meaning talk or conversation, follows.

Although the Jutlanders tend to be stolid, the people of Fünen easy-going and the Zealanders quite cosmopolitan because of their close contact with Copenhagen, the one thing that unites all Danes is their love of fun.

It is because of this love of pleasure that Copenhagen is known as one of the gayest cities of Europe. And for pleasure, Copenhagen begins and ends with the Tivoli Gardens, probably the most famous amusement park in the world. It offers everything in the field of entertainment—cabaret shows, dance halls, a pantomime theatre, symphony concerts, ballet, fireworks, games of chance, sideshows and restaurants of every type.

Whether you want simple amusement, a

Only boys between the ages of 10 and 16 can be members of the Tivoli Boy Guard. They are dressed in imitation of the King's Royal Guards, with bushy bearskins, elegant bandoliers, and carry musical instruments. Many of these boys join regular orchestras after the age of 16.

Day or night, Tivoli is always crowded in warm weather. Fountains add to its charm. In the background is the Royal Hotel.

Children enjoy a goat cart ride through the Tivoli Gardens.

spin on a merry-go-round or one of many other rides, or more serious cultural entertainment, you will find it at this beautiful park, resplendent at night with its more than 3,000,000 tinted lights. There are sweet scents and bright hues galore, due to the trees and flowers which grow in abundance along its walks and in its parks. Each day a special guard, composed of large, well-built boys in bearskins, marches through the garden past theatres, concert halls and the Tivoli's 25 restaurants. These range from small cafés where one can relax inexpensively over a cup of coffee and a piece of Danish pastry (here amusingly called "Vienna bread") to the Belle Terrasse, the Tivoli's most elegant restaurant.

This amusement park wonderland is open from May to September and was started more than a century ago by Georg Carstensen. He named it after the Renaissance gardens of Cardinal d'Este in Italy.

As we might guess from the magnificence of the Tivoli, the Danes love celebrations. Among their many holidays is Children's Day, held in May, which consists of shows, fairs, pageants, processions and dancing in the town square. May 4th is Liberation Eve, and candles can be seen glowing in every window to solemnly commemorate Denmark's liberation at the end of World War II.

Unusual as it may seem, the Danes also celebrate the Fourth of July. Theirs is the largest celebration of American independence outside of the United States. The ceremonies are held in Rebild National Park near Aalborg in northern Jutland, a site created by a group of Americans of Danish ancestry in 1912. They

The island of Fanö, off the west coast of Jutland, is famous as an international bathing resort. Many of the island's women still wear picturesque dresses decorated with bright buttons and belts and quaint caps tied with ribbons.

North of Copenhagen, along the coast called the "Danish Riviera," lies the large and rustic Deer Park (Dyrehaven), where 2,000 head of red and fallow deer are allowed to roam. This combination park and forest is a popular excursion place for Copenhageners the whole year through. Ermitagen, a small hunting chateau formerly used by the royal family, is located in Dyrehaven. There is also an amusement park and the excellent restaurant (shown here), Peter Liep's House.

bought and deeded the land to the Danish government with a proviso that it be the scene of an annual American Independence Day celebration. The Danes gather there for picnics, song-fests, speeches and concerts every Fourth of July.

The Danes work just as hard as they play. Despite the hardships that followed World War II, Danes have struggled to build their country to its present state of wealth. Now, for example, one-third of all families have telephones, and for 5,130,000 people, there are over 1,000,000 radios.

Over a million and a half of the population work in industry and as craftsmen. Twenty-eight per cent are engaged in agriculture. A nationwide cooperative system has enabled farmers to make a prosperous livelihood. Some farmers own their buildings, but rent the land from the state. In return, the state offers help with land reclamation, aids farmers financially and provides information and training in agricultural techniques. State loans assist the people until they can become independent farmers. Of the 200,000 farmers in Denmark, over 90 per cent own their own land.

Rent and food, the two major expenses of daily living, are low. However, a housing shortage makes it difficult to get an apartment or a house; tenants usually have to meet some sort of requirement, such as having lived in the township for a certain amount of time.

The fondest dream of many Danes is to own their own homes. Although the majority of Danes live in apartments, Danish apartments are modern, pleasant and have plenty of room. Most of them have either a balcony or a terrace. The Dane furnishes his apartment with high quality furniture. He buys it for lifetime use—even to pass on to his children.

For the past two centuries, Denmark has been working towards the elimination of class distinctions, aiming to give all its people more than an even share of the good things in life, providing they are willing to work for them. Men and women have equal legal rights.

There is one woman on the Supreme Court, one in the cabinet and 17 women are members of parliament. Women's privileges range from being admitted to holy orders in the Lutheran Church to smoking a man's cigar in public.

The vast majority of Copenhagen's one million population live in apartments, some in modern buildings such as these. Only a small number of inhabitants own their own houses.

Left: Our Saviour's Church in Copenhagen has an unusual steeple with an outdoor staircase, ascending to the spire. On the left is an apartment house in which each unit has a balcony.

Right: In the Christianshavn section of Copenhagen people still live crowded together in very old houses. With their peaked roofs, dormer windows and tall chimneys, these houses are reminiscent of days long past.

Right: In Denmark it is not unusual to see a woman smoking a cigar. This woman is on a ferry bound for Elsinore.

Left: In the city of Nyborg on the east coast of Fünen, nursery school children are called for and taken home in this unusual school "bus."

Below: Shown at her spinning wheel is an inhabitant of Manö. Since she has a flock of sheep, she does her own shearing and spins some of her own yarn.

Below: Fifteen families on the island of Manö have telephones. The operator works at home; she has had the switchboard installed in her bedroom.

Education at Denmark's three universities is free except for a small registration fee. Here, Danish girls talk to a professor in the University Hall of the University of Copenhagen, founded in 1479. The statue of Pallas Athene is the work of the Danish sculptor, W. Bissen.

EDUCATION

Denmark was one of the first countries to institute compulsory national education. Introduced as far back as 1814, the compulsory education act made Denmark the first country to become 100 per cent literate.

All children between the ages of 7 and 14 must attend school. Education is provided by state-supported schools and is free of charge. Parents may, however, have their children educated at private schools or by tutors, but all teachers and schools are subject to public inspection.

Up to the age of 11, children attend the primary school (*Folkeskole*). After that, they either remain in primary school until they reach 14, or they proceed to one of two types of high schools. The first type offers an academic curriculum (the classics, mathematics, languages and sciences), after which students who have successfully completed their exams may

proceed either to a commercial training school or to a 3-year Gymnasium offering a B.A. degree in preparation for university work. The second type of high school emphasizes practical subjects, leading to vocational training for apprentices in industry or handicrafts. There is no final examination and no degree is given.

Denmark has three free universities: the University of Copenhagen, founded in 1479; the University of Aarhus, established in 1933; and the new University of Odense, begun in 1964. In addition, there are technical colleges and 32 teachers' training colleges which maintain high and rigorous standards.

An outstanding feature of the Danish educational system is its Folk High Schools, instituted in 1844 by the poet, historian and bishop N. F. S. Grundtvig. His aim was to cultivate in young people, mostly those from rural areas, an interest in the vital problems of life and to provide them with an opportunity

Denmark's second university, the University of Aarhus, was established in 1933. Its modern buildings and campus spread over a hillside on the outskirts of the ancient city of Aarhus. The buildings are well equipped; in the university's laboratories Danish scientists work on important problems of nuclear physics.

to develop their special talents. Folk High Schools are for people who left the regular system at 14 and yet wish to continue their education while working. The study circle is much used as a method of teaching, and students do not take examinations. These schools are private institutions subsidized by the state. There are now 56 of them, the largest being the Danish High School in Askov. So effective is the principle behind the Folk High School in giving people with a desire for knowledge the opportunity to obtain it, that similar institutions have been founded throughout the rest of Scandinavia, in Germany, Great Britain and the United States.

Perhaps as a result of their fine educational opportunities, the Danes are avid newspaper readers. In this country, where illiteracy has been completely eliminated, there are about 200 newspapers of various kinds—a very large number in relation to the size of the population.

Henrik Dam, one of Denmark's outstanding scientists, has written several treatises on biochemistry. In 1943, he won the Nobel Prize for his work in medicine and physiology.

41

THE ARTS

The most popular Danish writers have been those who told whimsical stories with a clever point and perhaps a good moral. The best and the most famous was Hans Christian Andersen, a writer whose works, next to the Bible, have been the most widely translated in the world. *The Little Mermaid, The Red Shoes,* and *The Little Matchgirl* are only a few of the never-to-be-forgotten masterpieces that assure Andersen the immortality he so justly merits.

Right: Although Andersen is known mainly for his stories, he also made puppets, wrote plays for his homemade marionette theatre, and excelled in cutting delightful silhouettes out of black paper, such as the "Jumping Jack" pictured here.

Left: Hans Christian Andersen's childhood was marked by poverty and deep unhappiness. His parents quarrelled bitterly, and they were so poor that they slept on a bed made of planks which had previously been used to support coffins in the church. His imagination was Hans' only comfort, and he dreamed up beautiful stories which ever since have enchanted mankind. From his early youth, Andersen loved reading his stories aloud, both to adults and to children. This picture, taken in 1863, shows him surrounded by several rapt young ladies. Andersen died in 1875 at the age of 70.

The Little Mermaid who longed to be human is one of the most famous of Hans Christian Andersen's fairy-tale characters. Now immortalized in bronze, she watches over Copenhagen waters from a little promontory along the shore where children can play all around her.

Other masters of Danish literature are Christian Pedersen, known as the "Father of Danish literature," who translated the Bible during the first half of the 16th century; Ludvig Holberg, born in 1684, whose scathing satire created a new standard for Danish prose; the great historian and educational reformer, Bishop N. F. S. Grundtvig, who founded the Folk High Schools in 1844; and Sören Kierkegaard, born in 1813, whose influence on philosophy makes itself strongly felt today.

Throughout the second half of the 19th century, Danish literature was characterized by a great wave of realistic works. Important writers were Jens Christian Hostrup, Zacharias Nielssen, Jens Peter Jacobsen, Herman Bang, Carl Larsen, Carl Ewald and Henrik Pontoppidan.

The central figure in Danish literature after 1900 is Johannes V. Jensen, who was awarded the Nobel Prize in 1945 for his novel, *The Long Voyage*. Other contemporary writers are the three great B's—Baroness Karen Blixen, who wrote under the name Isak Dinesen and

Right: The most famous contemporary Danish author is the late Baroness Karen Blixen who wrote under the pen name of Isak Dinesen. Each of her books has been highly successful all over the world. Perhaps the best-known are "Seven Gothic Tales" and "Out of Africa," an autobiography which tells of her eighteen years in Africa. In her later years, Isak Dinesen went back to Denmark, living alone in her house situated halfway between Copenhagen and Elsinore. Her major works were written in English, not in Danish!

is probably the best-known Danish writer of this century, H. C. Branner and Karl Bjarnhof—and the lyric poet and novelist, Nis Petersen.

Danish drama dates back to 1722 when the first Danish-speaking theatre was opened in Copenhagen, but the most famous of Denmark's contributions to the theatre world is the Royal Danish Ballet. It was created under the direction of August Bournonville, the ballet master from 1829 to 1879. Under his gifted direction a first-class company was established; it has maintained its status ever since. The company has toured all over the world, and drawn enthusiastic audiences in many countries. The celebrated Royal Danish Ballet and Music

Dancers start their training early for the famous Royal Danish Ballet. They enter the ballet school at the age of 8. Leading roles are cast by seniority, and most dancers are at least 28 years old before being given a starring part. Here, a royal balletmaster trains youngsters on the roof of the Royal Theatre in Copenhagen.

The most famous ballet master of the Royal Danish company was August Bournonville, who wrote 50 original works, more than 10 of which are still performed. The productions of these ballets demand a special technique known as the "Bournonville style." This technique reflects the Danish character, for it expresses lighthearted gaiety and exuberance. Here Flemming Flindt soars through the air in a performance of "Bournonville Cavalcade."

Festival is held annually in Copenhagen at the end of May.

Denmark's largest theatre is the Royal Theatre in Copenhagen. The most modern is the Concert Hall at Tivoli. In addition, the city has 11 other commercial theatres. There are permanent theatres also in Aarhus, Aalborg and Odense. In the provinces are many facilities for the performances of touring companies. A particularly fascinating theatre is the courtyard of Kronborg Castle, Elsinore, the home of Shakespeare's Hamlet. Annual performances of *Hamlet* are held here, given by international

Kirsten Simone and Henning Kronstam appear in a performance of "La Sylphide."

At the Royal Danish Ballet, a ballerina adjusts the headdress of a colleague.

film industry. It is one of the oldest in the world. Since World War II many fine pictures, particularly documentaries, have come from Denmark, some of them winning top awards at international film festivals in various parts of the world.

companies. Kronborg Castle is the most appropriate of all theatres for a production of *Hamlet*, for the story on which Shakespeare's great play is based first appeared in the *Historia Danica* of Saxo Grammaticus, Denmark's first important writer. The tale of "Amleth" appeared in the folklore of Iceland some 200 years before it was recorded by Saxo Grammaticus near the end of the 12th century. Even today in Iceland, "Amlothe" means "fool." In northern Europe the story of Hamlet was so well known and so deeply rooted that it became a myth, but it did not reach England until the 16th century when Shakespeare used it as the basis of his masterpiece.

There is also considerable musical activity in Denmark. The Royal Orchestra is the oldest, having celebrated its 500th year of existence in 1948. The State Radio Symphony Orchestra is the largest in northern Europe.

Denmark's greatest modern composer is Carl Nielsen. Famous contemporary performers include Victor Schioler, Emil Telmnayl, and the late Danish-American opera star, Lauritz Melchior.

No discussion, however brief, of Danish arts would be complete without a word about the

The Royal Theatre of Copenhagen, opened in 1874, has one great advantage over other Danish theatres. By law, it is allowed prior right to produce any foreign play it wishes to stage.

Left: Of the many Danish artists who have illustrated Hans Christian Andersen's fairy tales, the first illustrator, Vilhelm Pedersen, is still considered the best. Here is one of his illustrations for "The Ugly Duckling."

Below: Boats bob placidly up and down in the canal that passes in front of one of Copenhagen's most fascinating places, the National Museum. Originally built in the 1750's for Crown Prince Frederik, the Museum offers visitors a tour through Danish history. Here is the world's finest collection of Stone Age tools. Also on exhibit are relics of the Viking past.

Above: A gala night at the Royal Theatre is marked by the attendance of the royal family.

Below: Statues of Danish dramatists Holberg and Oehlenschlaeger flank the entrance of the Royal Theatre. The late King Frederik, an accomplished musician and conductor, and the Queen attended frequently. The close personal interest taken by the royal family is a tradition dating back to the 18th century when the king gave the site of the present theatre to a group of players.

Modern art is not neglected in Denmark. Here is a room in the spacious modern art gallery called "Louisiana" situated just north of Copenhagen, on the shore of the Sound.

Below: Sculpture appears in many public places in all of Scandinavia. Here a group of sculpted cherubs gambol around a tree in Blaasgaards Square, Copenhagen. Kaj Nielsen, a renowned Danish artist, made this delightful piece.

Above: These amber figurines, dated 8000-5000 B.C., are the oldest known works of Danish art. Undoubtedly, they were believed to possess magical powers and to bring luck to a hunter who owned one of them. In ancient times amber was washed up from the North Sea onto the Danish shore— mostly of northern Jutland—in large quantities. During the Stone Age amber was widely used for trinkets and, in fact, was probably one of the country's principal barter commodities for procuring gold and bronze.

Right: Danish artists are always working to obtain beautiful shades and shapes in porcelain.

Shown here are handsome examples of Danish porcelain. Characteristic of all Danish handicrafts is a combination of functionalism and grace.

HANDICRAFTS

One excellent way to gain insight into the character of the Danes is to study the handicrafts which have developed during the past 150 years. Simplicity, restraint and elegance are the characteristics of their designs in silver, porcelain, textiles, furniture, ceramics, glass or pewter.

Among the scores of Danish handicrafts that may be purchased abroad, three special ones have achieved international reputations for distinction and quality: Jensen silver, Royal Copenhagen porcelain, and Danish furniture.

The most famous china service produced by the Royal Copenhagen factory is *Flora Danica*. Originally created for Russia's Catherine the Great, the service as a whole displays the botanical wealth of Denmark, each piece being decorated with an exact painting of a flower or plant. Once owned by the Crown, the Royal Copenhagen porcelain factory is now in the hands of private individuals.

Vases of all shapes and sizes, as well as tiles, take form with amazing swiftness under the skilled hands of Danish ceramists. The wares displayed here were made at a ceramic factory in the south of Zealand.

51

Danish glassware, like Danish porcelain, ceramics and stoneware, is internationally appreciated. This glass maker works on an exquisite, delicate vase.

Danish silverware is always associated with Georg Jensen, who established his foundry in 1904. He brought to his craft a sense of symmetry and won international acclaim for the refinement and subtlety of his designs. One of the special charms of his pieces is that he preferred dull tones to the shiny appearance of typically modern silver.

The beauty of Danish furniture gives it a prominent place among the nation's handicrafts. Its hallmark is comfort achieved with clean lines and grace, the special approach to form and space that has brightened countless households. Thanks to the special efforts of a whole group of designers, architects and craftsmen, these home furnishings of functional design and high-quality taste have been placed within the means of the average consumer.

Denmark has contributed to the comfort and beauty of households all over the world, daily reminding us of the ancient island kingdom which has become a peaceful, flourishing nation.

When designed and produced in Denmark, even a wooden chair is a work of art.

Denmark's soccer attracts the same wildly enthusiastic crowds as does soccer in Britain.

SPORTS

Denmark's national sport is soccer, and the defeat of the Danish team by Sweden (Denmark's greatest rival) would plunge the whole country into gloom. The sport has become so popular that 12,000 clubs have sprung up all over the country, with about 457,000 members, of whom 199,000 are active players.

Denmark has also been extremely successful in aquatic sports. The ready access to the sea and to the country's many lakes makes any water sport a natural for the Danes. Rowing, sailing and sculling are top aquatic sports, and Denmark has always been among the leading nations in these sports at the Olympic Games and other international competitions. The achievements of Danish women swimmers are also world famous.

Other sports the Danes enjoy are badminton, tennis, handball, archery, fencing, cycling, and the popular family sport, camping. Golf is also popular, and golf courses can be found in all the major tourist resorts.

July and August are the regatta months, when international contests take place along the Kattegat coast. Many people, even those with moderate incomes, own their own boats.

Above: During the last 20 years, camping has become extremely popular with the Danes. The countryside offers a magnificent choice of campsites, almost always close to either lakes or the sea. In summer, youth clubs and other organizations arrange camping trips. But many families set out independently in cars, or on bicycles, to spend a weekend by the sea or in a fragrant beech wood.

One of the most ancient of all occupations is still practiced in the Faroe Islands—whaling. The islanders seldom attack large whales, but concentrate their efforts on the pilot whales which travel in herds. The islanders head the whales into the bay where they capture as many as they can.

Next to Holland and New Zealand, Denmark stands third as an exporter of cheese. About 12 per cent of all milk delivered to the nation's dairies is used for making a variety of delicious cheeses. Danish "blue" is prized by gourmets everywhere.

5. THE ECONOMY OF DENMARK

The story of Denmark's national economy is an inspiring one, for this small country, poor in natural resources, has nevertheless achieved an impressive level of prosperity.

Only 80 years ago, Denmark's economy was in a critical situation. Its main export then was grain, but increased world competition had brought about a radical drop in prices. Desperately, the Danes searched for a means to survive. With profits from grain-growing wiped out, with only few dairy herds, with no natural resources to fall back on, a nation with less initiative might have given up. But the Danes set about to show the world that as long as there is no lack of will, there is always a way to do the best with what one has.

The 10th of June, 1882, marks the turning point in Denmark's economy. On that day at Hjedding, a small town in West Jutland, the first cooperative dairy processed the first milk brought in by local farmers. Denmark's cooperative farm program, which enables members to share costs and minimize the risk of loss to each individual, was on its way. After cooperative dairies came cooperative bacon factories, egg cooperatives, and the various

News of the dairy spread, and soon the cooperative farm program extended across the land.

As a result, Denmark has become one of the world's largest exporters of agricultural products. Danish butter, cheese, eggs, bacon and hams are known the world over for their high quality. To protect their own interests, the cooperatives see to it that "Made in Denmark" means the product is the very best that can be bought. The blue stamp of "Danish" on an egg, the *lur* symbol of Danish butter, the "Made in Denmark" stamp on a can of ham—all represent the same matchless quality as the name "Jensen" on a piece of silverware. Through cooperatives, the Danes, once faced with economic ruin, have met successfully the competition of much larger and much richer countries.

This glistening churn in a typical Danish cooperative dairy produces some of the finest butter in the world.

cooperative export societies with which Denmark has turned the threat of poverty into the prosperity it enjoys today.

AGRICULTURE

What exactly is Denmark's cooperative farm program? It was started by a young man named Stilling Andersen, a farmer living near Hjedding, who urged the local farmers to bring their milk to a central churning station for processing. The creamery was founded on the democratic rule of "one for all and all for one." Each cooperator had one vote regardless of the size of his farm. The advantage, Andersen pointed out, was that the cooperative could afford the most modern machinery and could hire expert agricultural consultants—advantages the individual farmer could never hope to have. Straightaway, the higher quality cooperative butter began commanding a higher price than that produced previously by individual farmers.

Danish eggs are marketed cooperatively through the Egg Export Association. Both weighing and grading are done carefully, and a system of stamping each egg makes it possible to identify the farm from which it comes. If a shipment should prove inferior, the producer is immediately warned. These methods of inspection and control have made the blue stamp of "Danish" synonymous with quality.

Shown here is a typical small farmer's holding. The Danish government assists farmers in many ways. It provides free education at agricultural schools, gives grants for the reclamation and improvement of soil and provides loans to farmers who wish to buy their own land. Although the farmer owns the buildings seen here, he put them up with the aid of a state loan, and pays rent for land, which is the property of the state.

Right: Agricultural schools give young farmers opportunities to learn the most up-to-date methods through practical training. In Denmark there are many agricultural schools, such as this one located at Odense on the island of Fünen.

Above: One of the most important annual events is the Livestock and Agricultural Fair at Copenhagen. Here are shown the country's prize farm animals—red Danish dairy cattle, Jutland, Frederiksborg and Belgian horses, and the Danish land race pig (of bacon fame).

One of Denmark's important exports is the working or draught horse. Pictured with his colt is the Jutland, a sturdy animal prized because of his adaptability to various climates and other conditions.

On a farm, everyone works. While his mother feeds the ducks and chickens, this Danish boy helps his father harness a team of horses to a cart.

The products of Denmark's farms and factories, along with items from all over the world, are marketed in the ultra-modern Rödovre Shopping Centre.

FISHING

Wherever you may be in Denmark, the sea is never far off. Fishing, therefore, is an important part of the economy. About 20,000 people are employed in the fisheries, and the fishing fleet, totaling 8,000 large and small vessels, brings in an annual catch worth many millions. Fishing is such an integral part of Denmark's way of life that in Copenhagen there is a monument of a fisherwoman dedicated to the women who preside over the city's fish market. This realistic, life-sized statue is called "The Unknown Fisherwoman."

The fish market is one of the major sights of Copenhagen. Here you can see how the fish literally come from the ocean straight to the table. They are brought up the canal in flat-bottomed boats like punts, which are moored side by side to form a series of watery cages where the fish are kept until wanted. The stalls are set up in the open air, and here the fisherwomen clean their fish. These women all come from the little fishing village of Skovshoved, a few miles from the capital; they still retain their traditional dress with full dark skirts and wear starched snow-white headdresses. Since national costumes have disappeared from most parts of Denmark, it is very charming to see these women dressed in the manner of their ancestors.

Above: The fish market along the Gammel Strand of Copenhagen retains a touch of charming provincialism. The market is tended by robust women, dressed for sitting outdoors all day. In the buildings on the right are several popular sea food restaurants.

Below: Two young Copenhageners prepare to sail their boats at Nyhavn, where the fishing boats come in.

Above: The Danish fisherman tends to be extremely self-sufficient. Although he probably sells his catch at a public auction shed (perhaps at the one shown here), he works from his own boat with a crew consisting of his sons or other relatives. Surprisingly few fishing boats are operated by companies. Like farmers, fishermen are assisted by government loans at low interest rates.

Hvide Sande is typical of northern Jutland's many small fishing towns. Denmark has only 14,000 professional fishermen, but they bring in an abundant catch of flat-fish, cod, herring, mackerel, eel, pike and others.

One of the few Danish manufacturing industries to obtain its raw materials from Denmark itself is the Portland cement industry. The main substances, clay and chalk, are found in enormous quantities along the east coast of northern Jutland, and big cement works have been built there, such as this one at Aalborg. The largest cement rotary kiln in the world is located here and revolves day and night without stopping.

MANUFACTURING

Some 850 of the world's cement factories use special machinery made in Denmark. Danish dairy equipment is sent to Argentina; Danish steam rollers to the Soviet Union; fishing cutters to India; special wood-burning locomotives to Finland; electric dry cells and batteries, head lamps and pocket torches to tropical countries. These products represent only a sample of Denmark's industrial exports, which now account for more than 25 per cent of its total exports. Although Danes have few raw materials of their own, they take those of other countries and turn out finished goods respected throughout the world for their high quality. A limited production of oil began in 1972, from Denmark's small sector of the North Sea oilfields.

OTHER PRODUCTS

On the lighter side of Danish products are three famous beverages: light beer, cherry brandy and *snaps*. The beer is the oldest of the three. Legends tell that the Vikings were especially fond of it and would drink it from the skulls of their enemies during victory celebrations.

Denmark's famous cherry brandy is world-renowned under its trade name Cherry Heering. It dates back to 1818 when a young Copenhagen merchant named Peter Heering was given a recipe for cherry liqueur by the wife of his employer. The formula is still a closely guarded secret and the business is now being carried on by the fifth generation of the Heering family.

The best-known Danish *snaps* is the Aalborg Akvavit, a pure white spirit made from a base of potatoes. More than 11 million gallons of it are produced per year.

This immense burnished copper cauldron is a feature of the Tuborg brewery, where about 3,000 men are employed. At Tuborg also is the largest kettle in northern Europe with a capacity of 345,000 bottles.

Typically Danish are the clean-cut lines of a new factory building at Aalborg, designed by Arne Jacobsen.

Motor car traffic in Copenhagen is now quite as heavy as in other world capitals, but there is still room for the ever-popular bicycle.

INDEX

64